The rabbit feels safe. He is near his home. If there is danger he goes down the hole.

Under the ground he feels safe. It is warm and dry in the home he has made. His enemies cannot easily find him. The fox cannot reach him there.

Look at the picture below.

1   What does the rabbit do when he is in danger?
2   Why does the rabbit feel safe?
3   Why can't the fox reach the rabbit?
4   Describe the rabbit's burrow.
5   Is the rabbit warm and dry?
6   Is the fox warm and dry?

The hole leads to the rabbit's home. The rabbit digs it deep under the ground. It is called a burrow.

3

Animal homes

Some rabbits are kept as pets. Their homes are not in the ground. They live in cages. A pet rabbit's home is called a hutch. Even Smokey can't get in there.

This is a pet rabbit's hutch. Look at the picture. Then copy out the sentences and fill in the blanks.

1 The ——— is in its hutch.
2 The hutch is made of ——— and ——— .
3 The roof is made of ——— and covered with ——— .
4 The rabbit's bed is made of ——— which keeps the rabbit warm.
5 The dish is for ——— . It is made of ——— .
6 The rabbit gets its water from a ——— .
7 Even when it rains and is cold the rabbit is ——— and ——— .

Oxford New Geography 1
a course for juniors
Gordon Elliott

Contents

Oxford University Press

Warm and dry

These chicks are with their mother. She is sitting on the nest. The chicks are playing around her.

They feel quite safe. When there is danger they can hide under her wings. They run to her for shelter. The heat from her body keeps them warm. Her wings keep them dry when it rains.

A rook's nest

A squirrel's drey

A robin's nest

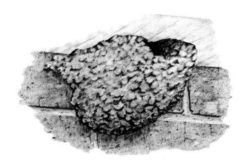

A house martin's nest

A badger's set

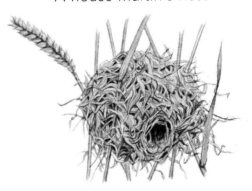

A fieldmouse's nest

Write out the sentences that are true.

1. Pet rabbits live in burrows.
2. Pet rabbits live in hutches.
3. Wild rabbits make their own burrows.
4. Pet rabbits make their own hutches.
5. A burrow keeps the rabbit cold and wet.
6. A hutch keeps the rabbit warm and dry.
7. A wild rabbit is usually safe in its burrow.
8. A pet rabbit is usually safe in its hutch.
9. One enemy of the rabbit is the cat.
10. All rabbits live in hutches.

These pictures show the homes of some birds and animals. Write some sentences about how the birds and animals keep warm and dry in their homes.

Our house

Wild rabbits make burrows to live in. We make hutches for pet rabbits. What about people? What do we do to keep warm and dry?

Most of us live in houses or flats. When it is wet or windy the house shelters us. In winter, when it's very cold, we need to keep warm inside the house.

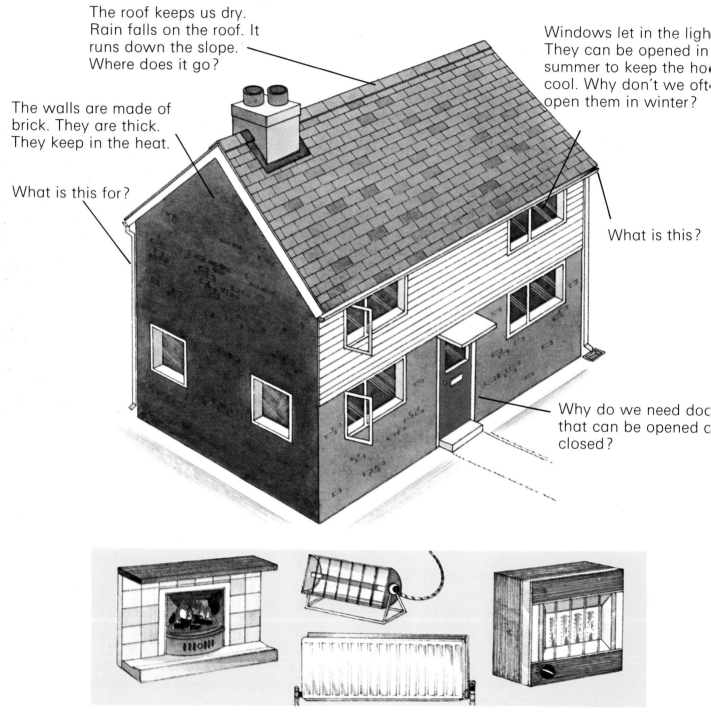

The roof keeps us dry. Rain falls on the roof. It runs down the slope. Where does it go?

Windows let in the light. They can be opened in summer to keep the house cool. Why don't we often open them in winter?

The walls are made of brick. They are thick. They keep in the heat.

What is this for?

What is this?

Why do we need doors that can be opened and closed?

Here are four ways of keeping the house warm. What are they? How is your house kept warm?

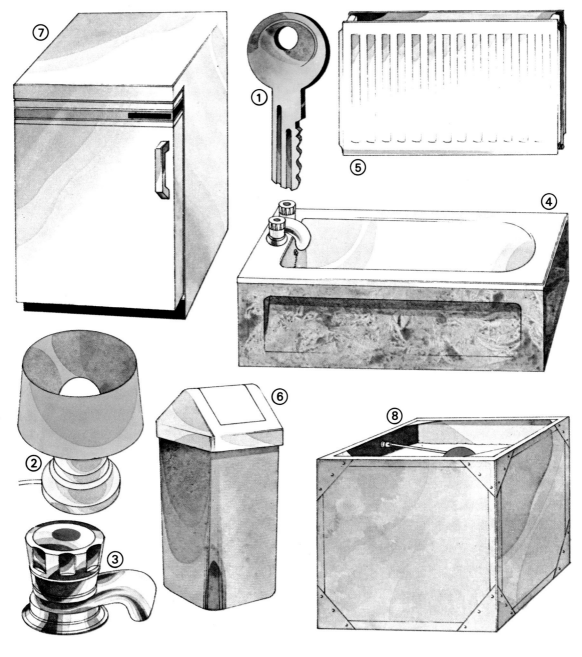

What are these things? They are all found in houses.

1 This is a ———. We open the door with it.

2 This is a ———. We switch it on when it gets dark.

3 This is a ———. We get hot water from it.

4 This is a ———. We use it for keeping clean.

5 This is a ———. It helps us to keep warm.

6 This is a ———. We put rubbish in it.

7 This is a ———. It keeps food cool and fresh.

8 This is a ———. Water is stored in it.

Which of these things are most important? Choose three and write some sentences about them to say why.

When it's wet

It is raining. Sara and Paul are running home. What is Paul wearing to keep himself dry? Is Sara dressed for rain?

Copy out and complete these sentences.

1 The boy playing cricket doesn't like the rain because ———.
2 The boy and girl on the beach don't like the rain because ———.
3 The farmer doesn't mind the rain because ———.
4 The fisherman doesn't mind the rain because ———.
5 The painter doesn't like the rain because ———.
6 We don't generally like the rain because ———.

How are these people keeping
dry? The words in the box may
help you.

> umbrella
> doorway
> hedge
> bus shelter
> tarpaulin
> milk float

1 The lady is carrying an
   ———.
2 The men are working under
   a ———.
3 Two people are standing
   in a ———.
4 The milkman is in his
   ———.
5 A boy is sheltering in a
   ———.
6 The girl is standing under
   a ———.

Checking

These are six enemies of the rabbit. The pictures and labels have been mixed up. Copy down the numbers and put the correct label next to each one.

1 Cat

2 Dog

3 Hawk

4 Adder

5 Crow

6 Stoat

Imagine you are a wild rabbit. A fox is chasing you. What would you do? Where would you go? How would you feel? Write some sentences using the words in the box to help you.

run	scared
fast	safe
hide	burrow

Copy these sentences. Use a word from the list below to complete each one. The first one has been done for you.

1 Birds live in nests.
2 Bees live in ——.
3 Foxes live in ——.
4 Dogs live in ——.
5 Horses live in ——.

burrows	kennels
stables	sacks
sets	nests
hives	shells
holes	dens

What am I ?

Write out the answers to these puzzles.

1   I am made of glass.
    I let in the light.
    If you look through me you
    can see the outside from
    inside.
    I am a ———.

2   I sit in a grate. You feed
    me with coal. When it
    gets cold I get hot.
    I am a ———.

3   Water runs down the roof
    into me. I am long, thin
    and hollow. When it rains,
    water rushes down me.
    I am a ———.

4   I open and close. Every
    house has several.
    Usually there is one at the
    front and one at the back.
    I am a ———.

Make up some **What am I ?**
sentences.

Look around

Look around your house or
flat and count:

1   how many windows there
    are;
2   how many doors there are;
3   how many are outside
    doors;
4   how many are inside doors.

Look around your school and
make a note of:

1   all the places where
    children shelter when it
    rains;
2   how the school is kept
    warm;
3   what the walls are made
    of;
4   what the roof is made of.

Puzzle picture

Look at the picture below.
What is it? Try making some
puzzle pictures yourself.

Playspace

1 Sara and Paul

3 Kay and George

2 John and Keith

Look at the pictures of children playing on the pavement. Write a sentence to say what is happening in each picture.

4 Lucy, Simon, Pete and Patrick

The first one has been done for you.

1 Sara and Paul are playing with a ball.

What is Bonzo the dog doing?

The pavement is not the best place for playing. Look at these pictures. Write a sentence to say what is spoiling the game in each picture.

The first one has been done for you.

1   The ball has gone into a garden.

Why do you think it is not a good idea to play in a street?

A park

Look at this picture of a park. Do you recognize the children? What are their names?

What games are the children playing? Complete the following sentences. The first one has been done for you.

1 Paul and Sara are fishing.
2 Kay and George are —— .
3 John and Keith are —— .
4 Lucy, Simon, Patrick and Pete are —— .

What is Bonzo the dog doing? Is the weather wet or fine? Is the wind blowing? What are the clues in the picture that tell you about the weather?

Paul and his friends like playing in the park. They can have a good time here. It is one of their favourite playspaces.

Look at the picture again.
Why do you think the children
like playing in the park?

Look back at the pictures on
pages 12 and 13. Write two
headings in your book. Call
them **In the street** and **In the
park**. Put each of the following
sentences under the correct
heading. One sentence could
go under either heading.
What number is it?

1　Cars get in the way.
2　There is plenty of space.
3　It can be very noisy.
4　Grown-ups get in the way.
5　There are swings and
　　see-saws to play on.
6　There are fish to catch.
7　Rain can spoil the game.
8　The traffic is dangerous.
9　There is not much noise.

Shapes

There are many interesting shapes in the park and in the street. This is a picture of what the pond would look like seen from above. It is round.

Look at the picture of the park. Make a list of things that are round.

Some things in the park and in the street are square or oblong. This is a picture of the hopscotch pitch seen from above. It is made up of a lot of small squares. Count them.

Make a list of things in the street and the park that are square or oblong.

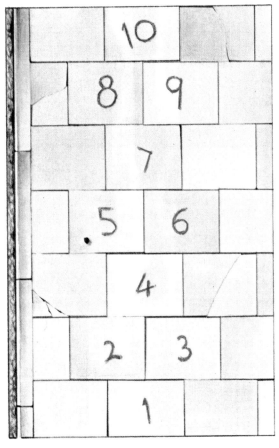

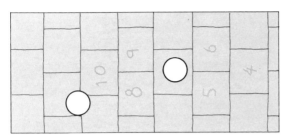

A plan of something shows the shape of it when seen from above. This is a plan of the pavement. We have put circles on it for children. The plan shows Sara and Paul.

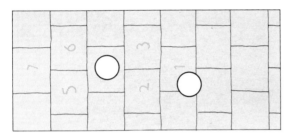

Look back at the pictures on page 12. Whom does this plan show?

Make a copy of this plan. It shows the see-saw. Add the children to your plan. What shape have you made them? Write the answer under your plan.

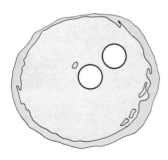

Look back at the picture of the park. Look at this plan. Whom does it show?

We can show other things by their shape. Write down the numbers 1 to 5. Next to them write what these shapes are. Choose your answers from this list: pavement, tennis court, football pitch, jar, fishing net.

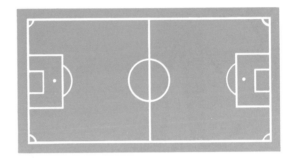

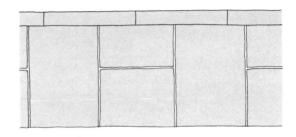

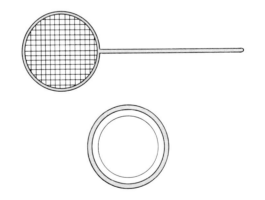

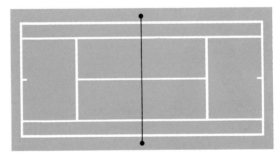

Now look around your classroom. Find some shapes. Draw them. Ask your friend to say what they are.

Tracks

Paul and Sara have been fishing for an hour. They have caught three fish. As they fish, they look around.

Paul spots some tracks in the mud. 'Look at these', he says. Sara comes over and bends down to examine them. 'I wonder what they are?' Sara says. 'I think we can find out. Let's follow them and see.

Sara and Paul begin to follow the tracks. The tracks lead across the mud and into some long grass.

Suddenly Sara shouts, 'Come here Paul. Look what I've found! This is what has made the tracks.' Look at the tracks. What do you think she has found?

Paul is lucky. He has caught four fish in the pond. He puts them in a jar. It is tea-time so he and Bonzo go home. When he gets home, Paul puts his fishing net and jar in the shed. He goes into the house for tea.

Look at the plan of Paul's house and garden. Look at the tracks Paul and Bonzo made with their muddy feet. Now read these sentences and copy out the ones that are true.

1 Bonzo followed Paul to the shed.
2 Paul went into the house through the front door.
3 Bonzo went straight to his kennel.
4 Bonzo went into the house through the back door.
5 Paul left the path once on the way to the shed.
6 Paul stayed on the path all the way to the shed.
7 Paul went from the shed to the back door.
8 Bonzo did not go into the house.

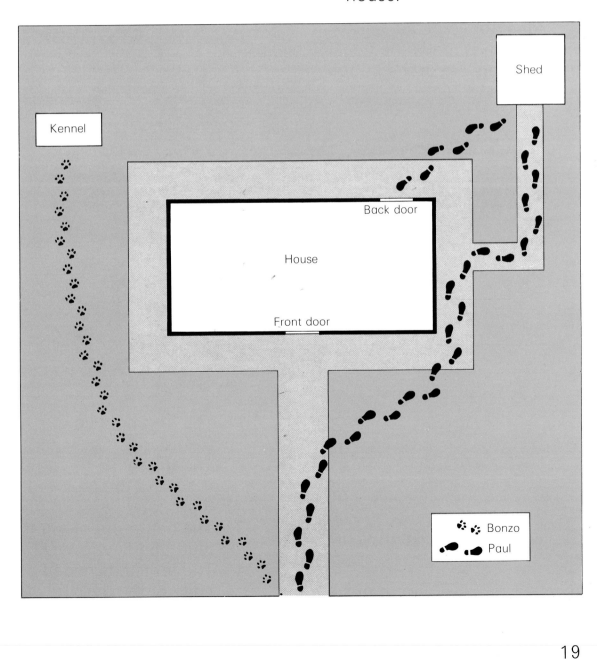

Checking

Did you guess what Paul and Sara found? This is what they saw.

Tracks can be fun. They can also give us clues. Look at the pictures of tracks. Write a label for each picture to say what has made the tracks. The answers are at the bottom of the page.

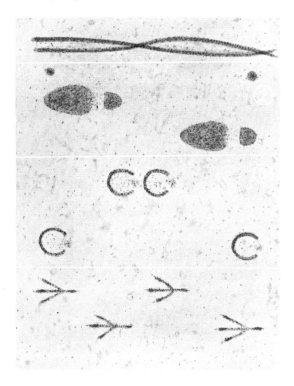

These are some puzzle pictures with tracks. Look at them carefully. Choose the correct sentence for each picture.

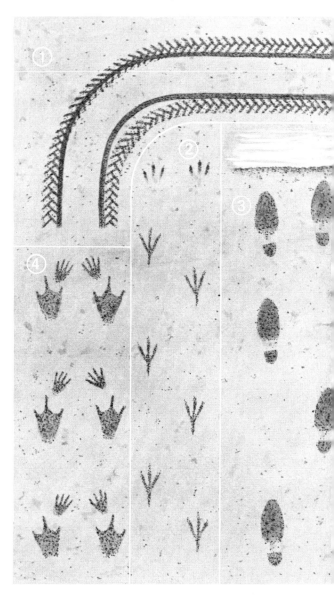

1   The frog hopped along the path.
2   The tractor went along the road and turned into the farm gate.
3   The heron ran along the mud and flew away.
4   The footsteps ended at the edge of the river.

Answers to tracks

1   Bicycle
2   Man with a walking stick
3   Horse
4   Bird

20

Look carefully at these pictures. Draw a plan of each object.

Look at this picture. It shows some handprints made 3,000 years ago. They were found in a cave in Australia.

Look at the shape of your own hand. Get a pencil and a piece of paper. Put your hand on the paper and draw round it. Cut round the outline. This shows the shape of your hand. Compare the size of your hand with that of your friend. Do the same with your foot.

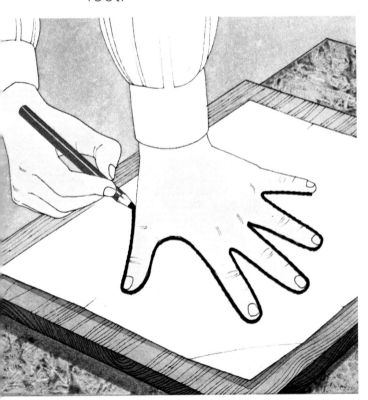

Draw the tracks that this man would make!

Look around

How well do you know your classroom? Class 1 are looking around theirs. They begin by sorting things into shapes. They look for things which have round plans. They look for things which have square or oblong plans.

Paul and Sara make a list of round shapes in the classroom. These are three things they find: football, apple, plate.

Look at the picture of the classroom. Can you see any more things that are round? Make a list of them.

George and John make a list of things that are square or oblong. Here are three of them.

Look at the picture on page 22. Can you see any more square or oblong shapes? Make a list of them.

Patrick is busy. He is making a list of where things are in the classroom. Patrick has started his list. Copy it out and finish it for him.

Now look round your own classroom. Make a list of:

1 things that are round;
2 things that are square;
3 things that you find on the floor;
4 things that you find on the wall.

Name: Patrick	
Floor	Walls
Table Floor tiles	Drawing pins Light switch

Write down five things in your classroom that are not round, square or oblong in shape.

Exploring the cab

Keith's father is a tanker driver. He drives a milk tanker. Let's look at the inside of his cab.

Copy out from this list things you can find in the driver's cab.

steering wheel   aerial
rubber mat   dashboard
headlight   seat
brake pedal   petrol cap
mirror   light
duster   clip board
windscreen wiper   tyre

These sentences tell us what some of the things in the cab are used for. The parts have got mixed up. Copy out the five **heads**. Then complete the sentences by giving each its correct **tail**.

Head	Tail
The steering wheel	is for holding pieces of paper.
The light	stops the lorry
The duster	is used at night to light up the cab.
The clip board	turns the wheels.
The brake pedal	is for cleaning the windscreen.

Which things shown in the picture might be used in other ways? Which things are only found in drivers' cabs?

These sentences tell us about the tanker. Some of them are wrong. Look at the picture. Then copy out the correct ones.

1   The driver's cab is at the front of the tanker.
2   The tanker is painted green.
3   The tanker has four wheels.
4   The tanker is used for carrying milk.
5   The tanker's number is HGY 746V.

What do these street signs tell the driver?

Look out!

The driver must keep an eye on children in the street. These pairs of sentences tell you why. Write out the correct one in each pair.

1   Children might run into the road.
    Children will not run into the road.
2   Children never cross without looking.
    Children sometimes cross without looking.
3   Good drivers are never careful.
    Good drivers are always careful.
4   Lorries can be dangerous.
    Lorries are never dangerous.

Look around the street

This is a busy street. It is in a town. The street is full of traffic. Cars, lorries and motor cycles speed along the road. They make a lot of noise.

Look at the signs and signals in the street. They tell people what to do. Some signs are for drivers. Who are the other signs for? The signs and signals are all different sizes and colours.

Look at the picture on page 26 and answer the questions.

1 How many cars are there?
2 How many lorries are there?
3 How many motor cycles are there?
4 How many cars are parked?
5 How many cars are moving?

Look and listen

Sue and Adrian are standing on the side of the road. They are watching and listening to the traffic. These are some words they have written about it. Make your own list of traffic words. We have started some to help you.

car	roar
v – –	screech
b – – –	wh – n –
l – r – –	hi – –

Look at the street signs and signals in the picture. Then copy out and complete each sentence.

1 The bus stop is near the —— shop.
2 The —— are at the crossroads.
3 The belisha beacons are on each side of the ——.
4 The —— sign is in the middle of the road.
5 The direction sign is near the ——.
6 The —— signs are in the middle of the zebra crossing.

These are some sentences about the street in the picture. Write the sentences choosing the correct words from those in brackets.

1 The street is very (busy, quiet).
2 The lorry is (quieter, noisier) than the car.
3 The lamp post is (bigger, smaller) than the traffic lights.
4 The lorry has stopped at the (traffic lights, zebra crossing).
5 There are (three, no) cars parked in the street.
6 The red car is driving towards (Oxford, Buckingham).

Are there any signs and signals in the street near your school? What do they tell you? Can you draw them?

Why did the chicken cross the road?

Because he saw the zebra crossing.

Watching things move

Paul has been asked to fetch a pile of books from the library. There are fifty story books, fifty readers, fifty atlases and fifty history books. Paul can only carry twenty books at a time. He puts the books into piles of twenty. How many piles are there? How many journeys will Paul have to make?

Paul finds a trolley in the library.

He loads all the books on to it. The trolley and the books are far too heavy for Paul to lift. But he can push the trolley quite easily. What parts of the trolley make it move easily? How many journeys will Paul have to make now?

Look around you, in the classroom, at home and in the street. Make a list of the different things you notice that have wheels. Write some sentences about them.

Look at these pictures. The woman is in a supermarket. She has to put her baskets down to take things off the shelves. The man is carrying a suitcase. It is very heavy. He can only move slowly. He is being pushed by people hurrying past him.

Now look at these pictures. How will the trolley help the woman in the supermarket? What is helping the man with the heavy suitcase?

Here are some more wheels. What has the smallest wheels? What has the largest? Write some sentences about each.

Checking

Shapes

This is a cup and saucer.

From the side it can look like this.

From above it can look like this.

This is a teapot.

From the side it can look like this.

Draw what the teapot would look like from above. Find some other things. Draw them from the side and from above.

What am I?

These are things you will find in a street. What are they?

1   My top is like an orange. I stand on a pole. I have a twin across the street.
2   I stand at the crossroads. I have three eyes. One is red.
3   I am made of concrete. I lie flat on the street. You walk on me.

Now draw pictures of each one. Label them.

Here are some more things you might find in the street. Make up some puzzle sentences for them.

Odd one out

Which is the odd one out in each of these sets? Write it down.

1   Car, bus, bicycle, traffic island.

2   Lamp post, bus, post box, traffic light.

3   Traffic warden, policeman, shop keeper.

4   Street, house, road, avenue.

5   Lorry, van, bicycle, car.

Ash Farm

Most of the food we eat comes from farms. Do you know what happens on a farm? Let's visit the Cook family at Ash Farm in Devon.

Harry Cook

Jean Cook

Nick

Alan

The family work as a team. They share many jobs on the farm and in the farmhouse. Jean looks after the hens and runs the home. Sometimes she has to drive the tractor as well, or milk the cows.

The farmhouse is near the road. Can you see the orchard at the side of the house? There are two barns and a milking parlour where the cows are milked. The other buildings are where the tractors and machines are kept.

The farm is a busy place as you can see. Mr. Cook has been shearing sheep. How do you know which ones have been shorn?

The dogs are keeping watch. Fly, Bess and Ben are collies. They do a lot of work on the farm. Bess and Ben are Fly's pups. They are two years old.

What other activities can you see?

Look at the picture. Copy out the sentences and fill in the blanks.

1 Mr. Cook is —— the sheep.
2 There are still —— sheep waiting to be sheared.
3 —— is feeding the hens.
4 Alan is putting a new —— on the tractor.
5 The poultry in the yard includes hens, —— and ——.
6 There are —— of hay in the Dutch barn.
7 Nick is loading the —— with sacks.

Would you like to live on a farm? Write some sentences to say why.

A busy day

It is seven o'clock in the morning. Mr. Cook has been at work for an hour. He has to milk the cows twice every day.

How many cows can you see? Do you think that cows have to be milked at weekends and during holidays?

It is eleven o'clock in the morning. Mrs. Cook has been in the fields for two hours. She is driving the tractor. The tractor is pulling a plough which is turning over the soil.

Why does Mrs. Cook need to wear warm clothes? Why are the gulls following the plough? Why do fields have to be ploughed?

It is three o'clock in the afternoon. Alan is driving the tractor. Mr. Cook and two of the dogs are riding in the trailer. They are going to collect the cows. It is milking time again.

How will the dogs help?

It is five o'clock in the afternoon. Mr. Cook has finished milking. He is mending a wall. Some of the stones have been knocked off by the sheep. They have made a gap in the wall.

Why must Mr. Cook always make sure that there are no holes or gaps in his walls and fences?

What time of year do you think it is? What clues are there to help you?

Gathering

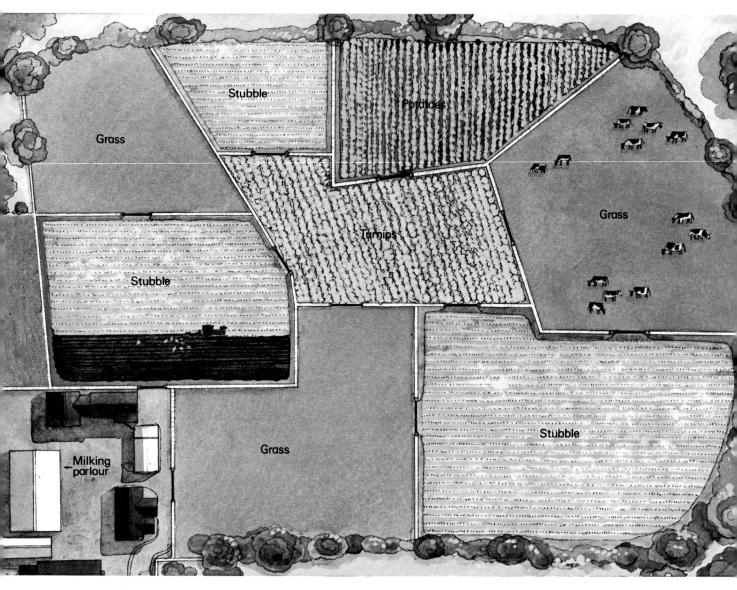

Twice a day Mr. Cook brings in the cows from the fields for milking. He is helped by Alan and the dogs.

The three dogs work together. Their job is to drive the cows across the fields and through the gates. Mr. Cook guides the dogs with a whistle. Sometimes he shouts.

Look carefully at the plan of the farm and answer the questions.

1 How many fields are there on the farm?
2 How many fields have crops growing in them?
3 What do you think was growing in the fields that now contain stubble?
4 Which two fields must the cows not go into?
5 How many gates must the cows go through to get to the milking parlour?

Look at the plans and the picture. Write answers to the questions.

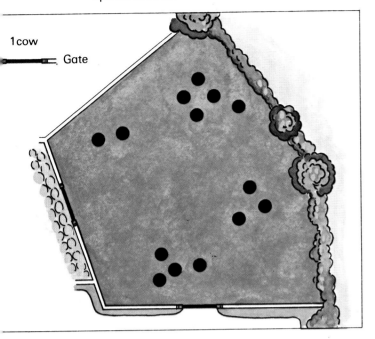

1 cow

Gate

1 How many cows are there in the field?
2 How many groups of cows are there?
3 Are the groups scattered or close together?

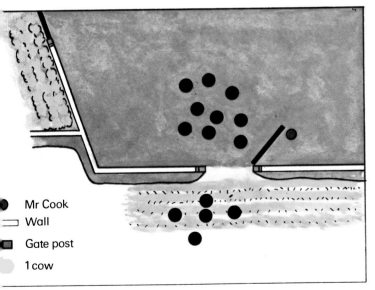

Mr Cook
Wall
Gate post
1 cow

4 How many cows are still in the grass field?
5 What is Mr. Cook doing?
6 How many cows have passed Mr. Cook?

7 How many cows have already gone into the milking parlour?

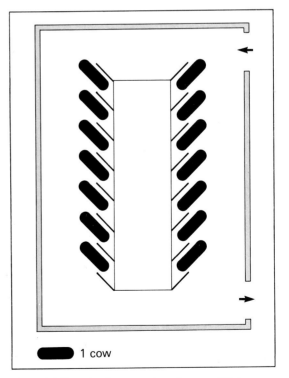

1 cow

8 What shape is the milking parlour?
9 Can all the cows be milked at once?

Milking

1 The cows go into the milking parlour one by one. Each cow goes into its own stall.

2 The cows stand side by side in their stalls with the milking equipment at their side.

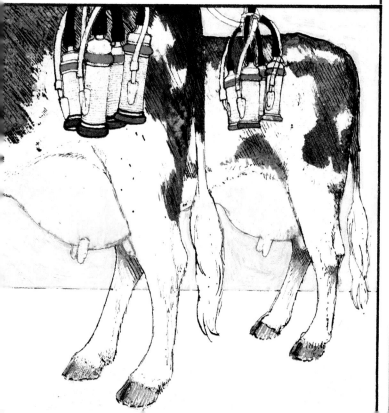

3 Mr Cook washes the cows' udders with warm water. The milk is then removed from the udders by machine.

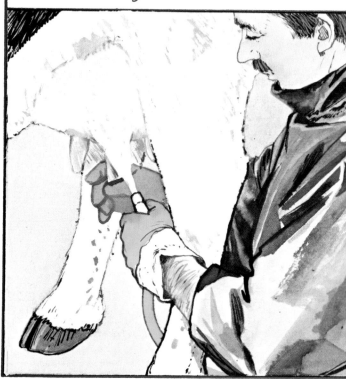

4 While the cows are being milked they are fed with concentrates. This is a special food which helps the cows to give a good supply of milk. After the cows have been milked, they are released from their stalls.

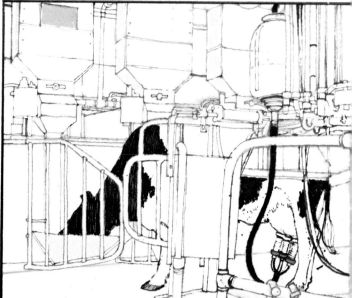

5 The milk from the cows is pumped into sealed jars and measured. It then travels by pipe to a large refrigerated tank.

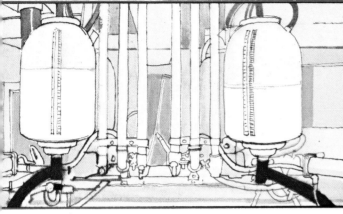

7 After milking, Mr Cook makes sure that the milking parlour is washed out with hot water to stop the spread of germs.

6 There the milk is stored until the milk tanker comes to collect it and take it to the bottling plant.

8 This picture shows how Mr Cook's grandfather used to milk the cows. Do you think the modern methods are better? Write some sentences to say why.

Produce

The three rows of pictures show you how wheat, apples and potatoes grow. One picture is missing from each row. Copy the chart. Choose the correct picture from the pictures at the side to fill the blanks.

	Spring	Summer	Autumn	
Wheat				
Apples				
Potatoes				

Look at this picture of Alan having his breakfast. Here are some of the things he will eat and drink.

orange juice   tea
sugar   milk
oats   toast
butter   bacon
eggs   mushrooms
tomatoes   salt
pepper

1 Which food is a cereal?
2 Which three things are drinks?
3 Which three things are not grown in this country?
4 Which things come from animals?
5 Which thing does not come from an animal and is not grown?
6 Which food is grown in greenhouses?
7 Which eight foods are grown or are made from things that are grown?
8 Copy out the list. Put a tick next to the things you like. Put a cross next to the things you do not like. Talk about your list with a friend.

All the products in the picture are animal products. Write down the four animal names and list their products.

These are pictures of things on Mr. Cook's farm. Can you draw what should go in the spaces?

A game

Nick has thought of a game with shapes. You could play it with your friend. Cut out a picture of a farm animal from a magazine.

Lay it on a piece of white paper and go round the cutout with dots. Show the dot picture to a friend and ask him to guess what it is. Now join the dots and give the animal its name.

Checking

The pictures show another busy day for Mr. Cook. It is a different time of year from that shown on pages 36 and 37.

Look at the pictures on this page and describe what is being done in each one. What time of year do you think it is?

Which jobs have to be done all the year round? Which are only done at certain times of the year? Use the pictures on pages 36 and 37 to help you.

These are some of the things grown in the fields at Ash Farm. What are they?

Look back at the plan on page 38. Which of these crops are not growing in the fields? Can you think why?

Which of these animals is not often found on the farm nowadays?

Why is the animal you chose no longer necessary on the farm?

Which of these objects are not used on the farm today?

tractor   gate
harvester   horse plough
milk churn

What has replaced them?

Which of these foods could Mr. Cook produce on his farm? Make a list of them.

The fire

1 Smoke is coming from the barn at Ash Farm.

2 Mr and Mrs Cook are not at the farm. They have gone into town to the market.

THE BARN IS ON FIRE. I MUST DIAL 999.

3 Alan is the first to notice the fire.

4 Five calves are in the shed next to the barn. Their lives will be in danger if the fire spreads.

5 Alan rushes across the farmyard. He opens the door of the shed.

QUICK, WE MUST SAVE THE CALVES.

6 As Alan enters the shed, four calves charge out.

7 The flames are now leaping across the roof from the barn. Alan finds the fifth calf huddled in a corner. It is too frightened to move.

8 How do you think Alan rescues the calf? Draw a picture and write an ending for the story.

The fire station

1 Alan's telephone call goes to the fire service's central control. The officer there phones the fire station nearest Mr Cook's farm.

2 The duty officer answers. He rings the alarm bell in the fire station. The firemen are alerted. It takes them two minutes to put their special clothing on and rush to the fire engine.

3 There are six men on the fire engine, including the driver. The engine roars. The huge doors of the fire station slide open.

4 The fire engine speeds out into the street with its siren wailing. The traffic in the street stops to let it pass. Some cars move out of the fire engine's way.

I WONDER WHERE IT'S GOING.

5 Mr Cook sees the fire engine race past him down the street.

6 At the farm the firemen see where the fire is and rush into action. They uncoil their hoses and switch on the pump. The water from the fire engine's tanks is pumped through the hoses and sprayed on the flames.

7 When the tanks are empty, the firemen use the pump to suck up water from the farmyard pond.

8 It takes an hour to put out the fire. The barn is now a charred ruin but at least all the animals are safe.
As the firemen are leaving, Mr and Mrs Cook drive into the farmyard. Imagine you were them. What would you see? How would you feel? What would you do? Talk about it with a friend.

Rescue

Firemen do not spend all their time putting out fires. Have you ever thought about other jobs firemen do? They can use their skills and equipment in many different ways to rescue people and animals in danger.

In each of the pictures on page 51 the firemen will have to use special equipment in the rescue. Look at the pieces of equipment below. Decide which piece will be used in each rescue. Write some sentences for the pictures opposite to describe what the firemen will do. Say how the equipment will be useful.

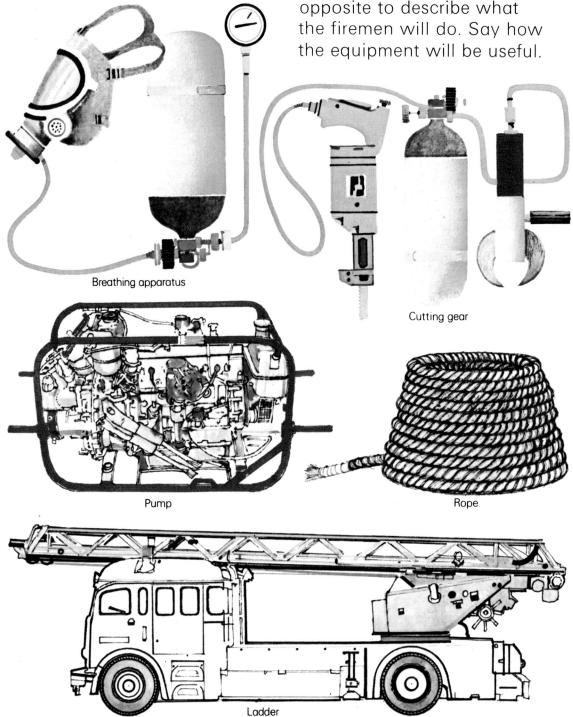

Breathing apparatus

Cutting gear

Pump

Rope

Ladder

1 A cow has fallen into a ditch and is unable to get out.

2 There has been a leak of poisonous gas. A man has been overcome by fumes.

3 The window cleaner's platform has got stuck.

4 There has been a motor accident. The driver of the lorry is trapped in his cab.

5 The houses have been flooded with water from the river.

Checking

Water

When the firemen arrived at Ash Farm they needed water to put out the fire. Where did they get it from?

From where else might the firemen have got water? They could have looked for a sign like this.

The sign tells the firemen that there is a pipe from the water-main there. They can attach their hose to the nozzle and use the water to spray the fire. Find out what the sign is called. Are there any near your school? Draw one.

What happened when Alan dialled 999?

The operator asked him, 'Which emergency service do you want?' What would Alan say? What other information would he give to make sure he received help? Imagine you are Alan. Write down what you think he said on the telephone.

Puzzle corner

How did the barn catch fire? What do you think happened? The picture gives you a clue.

A story

The day after the fire, Mr. Cook told Nick about the last big fire at Ash Farm. It happened before Mr. Cook was born. In those days hay was kept outside. It was stacked in huge piles called hay ricks.

One night, one of the hay ricks burst into flames. In no time there was a great blaze. There was no telephone on the farm so one of the men had to ride down to the village. He used the telephone at the doctor's house to call the fire brigade.

While they were waiting for the fire engine to come, everyone tried to help put the fire out. They formed a long chain. Buckets of water from the pond were passed along the chain and thrown on the fire. Some men tried to put out the flames with old blankets.

The fire lit up the farmyard. Sparks flashed everywhere. The animals were very frightened but they were all led out of danger.

By the time the fire engine arrived, one hay rick had been destroyed. It took the firemen several hours to put the fire out.

Write some sentences to describe what you think the farmyard looked like the next morning. Draw some pictures to illustrate your sentences.

FIRE! FIRE!

In the Town

| 8 | 9 | 10 | 11 | 12 | 13 | 14 | 15 | 16 | 17 | 18 | 19 | 20 | 21 |

For this game you need dice and counters. Two or more can play. Make a score card before you start.

Rules
1. Start in the town.
2. Throw the dice in turn.
3. If you land on a shaded square look at the penalty board.
4. Fill in the score card as you play.
5. When you finish the Town board move to the Country board.
6. The lowest scorer is the winner.

Left column (top to bottom): 7, 6, 5, 4, 3, 2, 1

Right column (top to bottom): 22, 23, 24, 25, 26, 27, 28

Bottom row: 40, 39, 38, 37, 36, 35, 34, 33, 32, 31, 30, 29, 28

In the Country

| 40 | 1 | 2 | 3 | 4 | 5 | 6 | 7 | 8 | 9 | 10 | 11 | 12 | 13 |

Left column (top to bottom): 39, 38, 37, 36, 35, 34

Right column (top to bottom): 14, 15, 16, 17, 18, 19

Bottom row: 33, 32, 31, 30, 29, 28, 27, 26, 25, 24, 23, 22, 21, 20

How to make a score card

Square number	Penalty	Square number	Penalty

Total

Penalty board

Penalty **10** points

Penalty **5** points

Penalty **20** points

Penalty **10** points

Penalty **5** points

Penalty **5** points

Penalty **10** points

Penalty **10** points

Penalty **20** points

Penalty **5** points

Penalty **5** points

Penalty **10** points

Penalty **20** points

Penalty **5** points

Penalty **5** points

Hill View Farm

This is the McAdams' farm in Scotland. You can see Mr. McAdam in the picture. He is going into the barn to load some bales of hay on to the trailer. Glenn and Annie, the sheepdogs, are sitting by the landrover. They are waiting for Mr. McAdam.

Angus the shepherd is very busy. He is looking after three lambs. It is February and lambs are usually born on this farm in April. These three are early.

One has lost its mother. Angus has put them all in a covered pen. It is lined with straw. The lambs will be warm and dry in there.

Five quick questions

1 How many animals are in the picture? Make a list of them.
2 What job does Angus do?
3 What crop is stored in the barn?
4 Why is the pen lined with straw?
5 What job will the sheepdogs do on the farm?

It is February which is a cold month in Scotland. It is colder up on the mountain and there is usually more snow there than near the farm.

Snow has barely covered the grass in the fields near the farm. Up on the mountain the snow is deep. A strong wind has piled it into drifts.

Mr. McAdam and Angus are worried. Many of their sheep are up on the mountain. They are afraid some might be buried under the snow.

Look at the pictures on these pages.

1 Make a list of clothes Angus is wearing. Why is he wearing warm clothes?
2 Why does Mr. McAdam have to take hay to the sheep?
3 How do the sheep on the mountain keep warm?
4 Who is helping to collect the sheep?

5 What can you see in the back of the trailer?
6 How do Mr. McAdam and Angus find the buried sheep?
7 How do they get them out of the snow?
8 Why is Mr. McAdam taking some sheep back to the farm?

The orphan

One of the sheep has died in the snow. It left a new born lamb. What will Angus do with the lamb?

These things will be used to look after the lamb until it is strong. What are they? Write a sentence for each one to say what it is used for.

A busy day

It is nine o'clock in the morning. This is a field near the farm. Mr. McAdam and Angus have brought some sheep here from the mountain. Most of them have lambs. They are kept near the farm because it is not as cold there as on the mountain. Angus can also get to the sheep more easily. He needs to look after the weak and sick ones.

Angus has been up all night. Can you think why? What are the clues in the picture that tell you it is spring time?

It is afternoon. Mrs. McAdam is driving the tractor. She has been working in this field for two days. When the field is ready they will plant some barley. It will grow during the summer. In September it will be cut. The straw will be useful.

What is Mrs. McAdam doing? How can you tell she has nearly finished? Why must she be very careful in this field? Why is she wearing a helmet? What will the straw be used for?

Angus is checking the sheep on the mountain. He has brought Glenn with him. He is going to give two sheep some medicine. They are sick. He is worried because a stray dog might attack the sick sheep.

Where is Annie? What is Angus doing? What are the white patches? Why are they near the wall? What other animal might attack the sheep?

Mr. McAdam and Angus are back at the farm. They are talking to the lorry driver. He has brought a load of hay and straw. Mr. McAdam and Angus will put it in the barn to keep it dry. Mr. McAdam is paying the lorry driver for his load.

How will they unload the lorry? What will the hay and straw be used for? What things could Mr. McAdam sell to earn money to buy hay and straw?

Use the pictures to write a diary. Call it **A day on the McAdams' farm**.

Gathering

It is a hot summer's day. Angus is standing by the gate. He is working with Annie and Glenn. You can see them on the cliff. They are collecting sheep from the mountain and driving them to the field near the farm.

It is a difficult job. Angus and the dogs work as a team. They help each other.

Signals

Angus guides the dogs by whistling. Each whistle is a signal. The dogs know exactly what to do when they hear it.

1   A long whistle means the dog has to turn to its right.
2   A short whistle means the dog has to turn to its left.
3   A long whistle followed by a short one means the dog should go straight ahead.

Imagine you are Angus. Look at the picture and copy down the letters. What signal would you give to the dogs when they reached each spot?

At the end of the day the sheep are taken back to the mountain. Angus signals to the dogs from the same place. Copy down the letters, beginning with **G**, and put the correct signal next to each one.

60

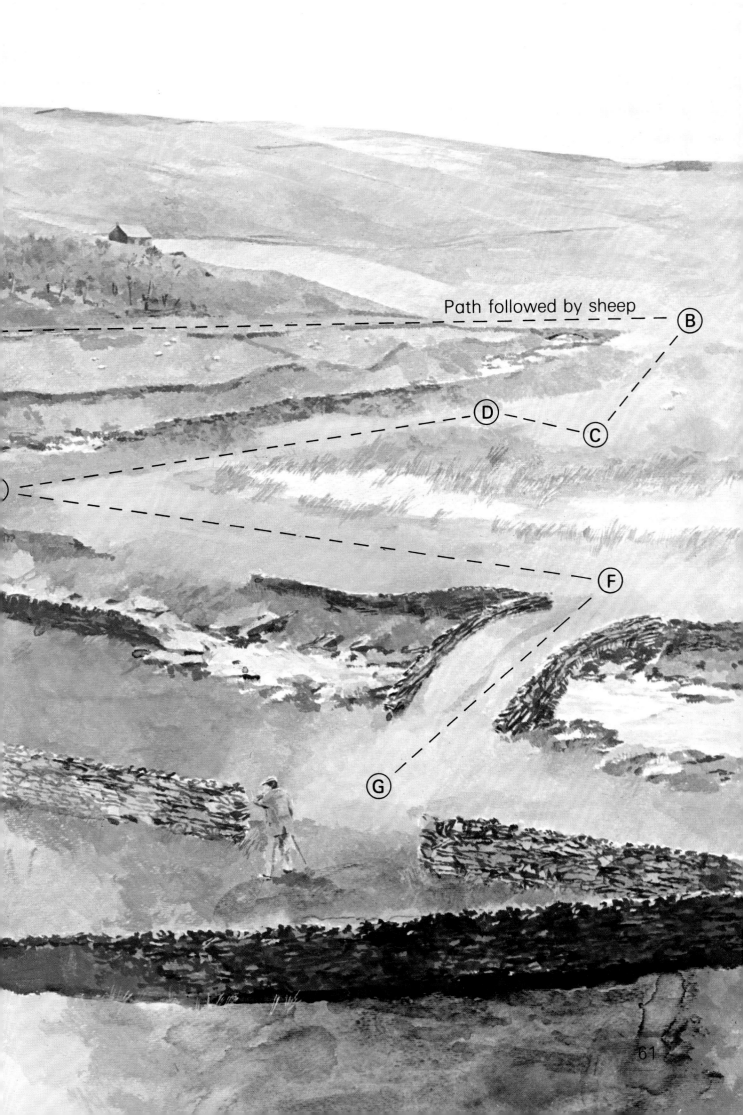

Path followed by sheep

B

D C

F

G

Shearing

Every summer the sheep on Mr. McAdam's farm have their wool clipped. This is called shearing. Four or five farmers help each other at shearing time. In this way the job is done more quickly.

Each man uses electric shears to cut the wool. He grips the sheep between his knees to keep it still. It is hard work but the sheep seem glad to get rid of their thick coats.

After they have been sheared the sheep have to be dipped. They are pushed into a trough filled with water to which chemicals have been added. This kills all ticks and grubs that may live in the sheep's coat and be harmful to it.

The men are shearing. Their wives are busy preparing food and drinks. They make sandwiches, cake and tea. These soon disappear as the men are hungry and thirsty.

The wool from each sheep is called a fleece. All the fleeces are piled together on large pieces of sacking. When there is a big pile the sacking is made into a bundle and tied.

Can you see the wool merchant's lorry waiting in the farmyard? It is being loaded with the bales of wool. A large tarpaulin is pulled over the load and tied with ropes.

Complete these sentences.

1   Each summer the sheep on Mr. McAdam's farm are ———.
2   The men use——— to clip the sheep's wool.
3   A sheep's wool is called its ———.
4   Shearing is done in early summer before it gets too ———.
5   After shearing, the sheep are ———.
6   The water is mixed with ——— to kill ——— and ———.
7   Before they are sheared the sheep look ———, afterwards they look ———.
8   The fleeces are wrapped in ———.

9   The wool is bought from the farmer by a ———.
10 A ——— is used to keep the wool dry on its way to the mill.

What am I?

Do you know any other sayings or poems about sheep or lambs?

Checking

An arrow plan

Angus drew a plan. It showed how he brought in the sheep from the mountain. He did not finish it. Make a copy of the plan and finish it by adding more arrows and boxes E, F and G. Look back at pages 60 and 61 to help you.

Snowstorms

Every year Mr. McAdam hopes the snow will not be too heavy. In a bad winter he loses a lot of sheep in the snow drifts. The chart shows what happened in February 1980.

	Sheep lost 1980	Weather	Sheep lost 1981	Weather
Week 1	5	heavy snow		
2	2			
3	0			
4	2			
Total	9			

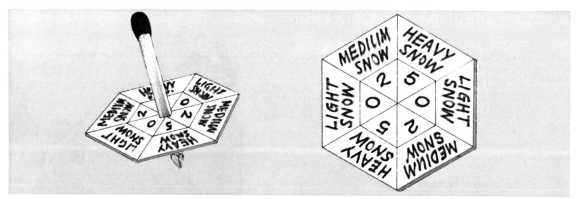

Make a spinner like the one in the picture from a piece of cardboard. Copy out the chart. Then do four spins, one for each week in 1981. Fill in the blanks on the chart. How many sheep did you lose in 1981? Was it a worse or better year than 1980?

More arrow plans

Make some simple arrow plans to show how you go from your

1 desk or table to the classroom door;
2 classroom to the cloakroom;
3 classroom to the school gate.

Make some more arrow plans. Show them to your friend. Give him or her some clues. See if your friend can work out what your arrow plans show.

Comparisons

Make a copy of the chart. Find the answers and put them in the spaces. Some have been done for you.

A gathering game

It is best to play this game outdoors or in your school hall or gym.

Pick ten children from the class. Choose seven of them to be sheep, two of them to be sheepdogs and one of them to be the shepherd.

The sheep are sent off but must keep in a group. The shepherd whistles to the dogs using the same signals as Angus did. The dogs must obey the signals and drive the sheep back to the shepherd. The rest of the class decides whether the shepherd and his dogs work well together.

	Ash Farm	Hill View Farm
1 In which country is the farm?	England	page 56
2 What chief animals do they keep?	page 36	page 57
3 What do they get from them?	page 36	page 62
4 What other animals do they keep?	page 35	page 59
5 What machines do they use?	pages 34, 36, 40	pages 56, 58, 59
6 Is the land flat or hilly?	page 36	page 58
7 What crops to they grow?	pages 38, 42, 49	page 58

Links

Andy's football was kicked into the water. Andy thought he had lost it. Each gust of wind blew the ball further away. But it was saved by Andy's friends. They joined hands to make a chain. Each child was a link in the chain. They gripped each other's arms and ran into the water. Keith was the last link in the chain. He reached out and rescued the ball.

Look at these pictures. Each shows an example of a **link**.

Copy out the sentences and finish each one.

1   The chain has —— links.
2   The dog is linked to the boy by its ——.

Missing links

In the first picture the man is climbing a ladder. In the second picture the ladder is missing. Look at the other pictures. What is missing? Write a sentence for each picture. Begin each sentence **The missing link in this picture is** ——. Draw some missing link pictures of your own. See if your friend can guess what is missing.

There are many different kinds of links. Copy out and finish these sentences, using the words in the boxes. The pictures will help you.

1 The men ——— on the ———. One man ——— his ——— into the other man's legs.

> links, swing, arms, trapeze

3 Paul is playing a jungle game. He has tied a ——— between two trees. It ——— the trees and he uses it to ——— the gap.

> cross, rope, links

2 Bonzo is on the far ——— of the ———. Sara crosses over the ——— to fetch him. The bridge links the two ——— of the canal.

> canal, sides, bank, bridge

4 This track ——— the ——— to the road. The ——— tanker goes along it.

> farm, links, milk

Getting to school

Keith lives at 5 Bridge Road. Find his house in the picture. Every day Keith walks to school. It is not very far. How long do you think it takes him?

Sara and Paul live in New Street. You can see them in the picture. They are just leaving their houses.

Keith walks along Bridge Road and down New Street to get to school. He often meets Sara and Paul on the way.

Trace Keith's journey to school in the picture. When he is late, Keith takes a short cut. Find it in the picture.

Five quick questions

1. At what number Bridge Road does Keith live?
2. Who lives furthest from school?
3. Who lives nearest school?
4. Does Keith pass Sara's house when he takes the short cut?
5. Who would usually get home first from school?

68

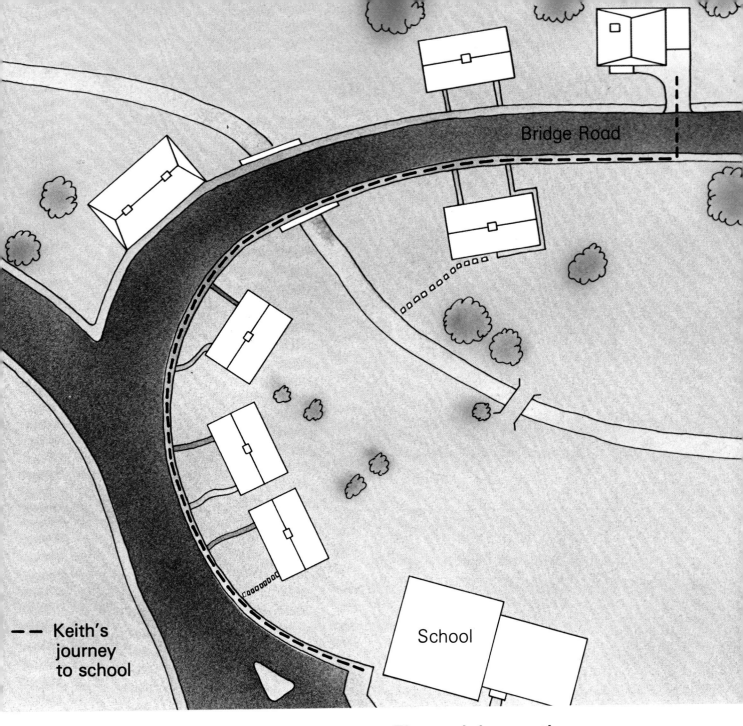

Bridge Road

– – Keith's
journey
to school

A plan

The plan above shows Keith's journey to school. Make a copy of it. Colour Keith's house red. Add the path Keith uses for his short cut to school. Show Sara's journey to school on your plan.

Five quick questions

1 How many houses are shown on the plan?
2 Is the school bigger or smaller than Keith's house?
3 What is missing behind the school? Add it to your plan.
4 Which road name is missing? Write it on your plan.
5 How do you think Keith's road got its name?

The postman's round

Mr. Burns is a postman. He begins work at seven o'clock in the morning. He goes to the post office on his motor cycle. The journey to work takes him half an hour.

His first job is to sort the letters for his round. It takes Mr. Burns about an hour to do this. He puts them in bundles in his bag.

In winter Mr. Burns carries a torch on his round because the mornings are dark. He does not like winter. It is usually cold and sometimes wet. The paths are often slippery if there is frost or snow. This slows him down. He likes the summer better. Can you think why?

Ten quick questions

1 What time does Mr. Burns leave home for work?
2 What time does he start his round?
3 What slows him down in winter?
4 Would he finish his round earlier in summer or winter?
5 Are the mornings lighter in winter or summer?
6 Which house is Mr. Burns going to?
7 What is he taking to this house?
8 Why does Mr. Burns use a bicycle?
9 How much does it cost to send a letter in England?
10 Would it cost less or more to send a large parcel?

Mr. Burns is going to 10 Westland Road. What is he delivering?

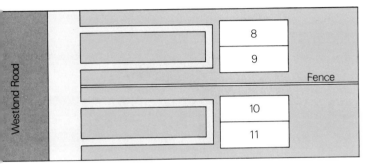

This is a plan of part of Westland Road. Copy it and mark on Mr. Burns's round.

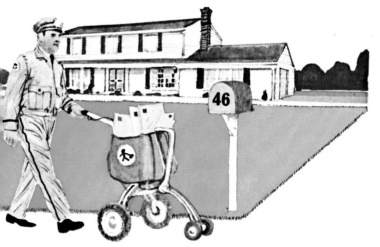

A postman is delivering letters to houses in an American town. Write down the things that are different from an English town.

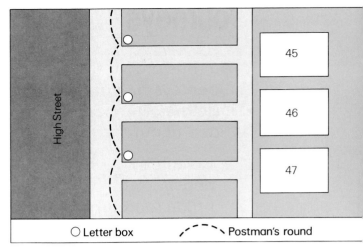

○ Letter box   ⌐ ⌐ ⌐ Postman's round

This is a plan of part of an American town. Is the postman's round different from Mr. Burns's round? Why?

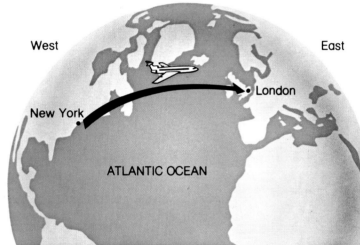

The diagram shows the journey of a letter by air mail from America to Britain. The aeroplane flies from New York to London. It takes six hours.

1   What ocean does the aeroplane cross?
2   In what direction does it fly?
3   Could letters be sent from America to Britain by ship?
4   Would the journey by ship be faster or slower than by air?

71

Journeys

Keith has drawn five pictures of journeys he has made. These are sentences he has written about them.

1 I went for a walk with my dog.
2 I rode round the block on my bike.
3 We went along the canal on a barge.
4 I caught a bus to the park.
5 I ran to the shop.

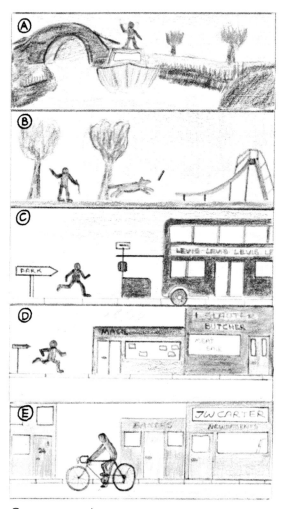

Sort out the sentences to match the pictures. Sentence **1** goes with picture B. Write answers for the rest.

Ways to travel

Copy down the three headings:

On land
By water
By air

Look at the five pictures. Put the letter for each under the correct heading. Think of other ways to travel. Write each one under the correct heading.

Hand signals

This picture shows Keith giving a hand signal. What does it mean? Do you know any other hand signals? Draw them. Write a sentence under each drawing to explain what the signal means.

Signs

This is a sign Keith saw at the side of the road. What does it mean? Draw some of the road signs you pass on your way to school. See if your friend knows what they mean.

Journey of a letter

The pictures show the journey of a letter. Use the pictures to write a story. The words under the pictures will help you.

Post box, red, stamp, letter.

Postman, van, collect.

Post office, sorter, piles of letters.

Railway station, mail bags, platform,　train, loading.

Unloading, Hull, van, postmen, trolley.

Post office, van, mail bags, letters.

Sending messages

A letter is one way of sending messages. Here are some other ways. What are they? For each picture say whether you would (a) see the message; (b) hear the message.

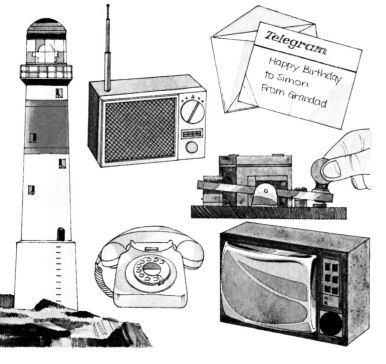

Whispers

Try this game in your class. One person makes up a short message of about six words. He or she whispers it to a neighbour who passes it on to the next person. The message is passed round the class by whispers. The last person tells it to the teacher who puts it on the board. Was it the message you started with? If not, try another. This time make it shorter. If the message was right, try a longer one. Does the class improve with practice?

Bees

Bees give messages to each other. A bee leaves the hive to look for flowers. When it flies back it does a dance. This tells the other bees where the flowers are.

Puzzle corner

People use pictures to tell each other things. A builder has done some work for Mrs. Thomas. He has sent her the bill. Instead of writing it, he has drawn some pictures. Mrs. Thomas has written what she thinks the bill says. Do you think she is right?

Two men   for three days

building a wall   cost £50

Make up some picture messages of your own. See if your friend knows what they say.

74

More signs

The pictures show some more signs and signals. Write some sentences about each. The words in the box will help you.

cat, angry, blind man, white stick, tapping, lamp post.

What would you do if . . .

you were driving along in a car and you saw sign **1**; you were driving along a motorway in a fast car and you saw sign **2**?

Crawler lane

Codes

The letter on page 71 has this at the bottom of the address: **HU10 7PJ**. Find out what it is called. Is there one for your house? What is it?

Sara lives in Manchester. She is telephoning her friend in Liverpool. First she dials 051. This is the code for Liverpool. Find out the codes for Manchester and London. What is the code for your area?

This is a car number plate. It is a kind of code. Find out what the letters on a number plate mean. The last one is a clue to the age of the car.

What other codes can you find out about? Make a list of them. Here are clues to two codes.

Puzzle corner

Can you 'say' these without using words?

1 Yes
2 No
3 What time is it?
4 I want a drink.
5 Go away.

Make up some more yourself. Try them with a friend.

Checking

Make a copy of the heading **My journey to school.** Then answer the questions.

1 Do you live near school or a long way away?
2 How do you get to school?
3 Do you cross a road on your way to school?
4 Do you pass any shops?
5 Are the roads busy when you go to school?

Draw a picture to show how you get to school.

My class

Find out from your class

1 who lives nearest your school;
2 who lives furthest from your school;
3 how many children walk to school;
4 how many come to school (a) by bus; (b) by car.

Trip diary

On 16 August Sara went in her father's car to see her aunt. The trip meter shows how many miles they travelled.

This is Sara's diary. She has been keeping notes of all her journeys for a week.

Date	Trip	Travel
10 August	Went to shops	Walk
11 August	Took Bonzo to vet	Bus
12 August	Went to ice rink	Walk and bus
13 August	Dancing lessons	Walk
14 August	Stayed at home	
15 August	Went to park	Walk and bus
16 August	Went to visit aunty	

1 How many times did Sara go by bus?
2 How did she travel on 16 August?
3 How many miles did she travel on 16 August?
4 How far is it to her aunt's house?
5 Was Sara at school or on holiday during the week?

Make your own trip diary. Talk about it with your friend.

The post box

Each post box has a notice like this on it. It tells you when letters are collected.

1 What time is the first collection?
2 What time is the last collection?
3 How many times are letters collected each day?
4 If Keith went to the post box at 3 o'clock, what time would his letter be collected?
5 Are letters collected every day from the box?

Journey of a letter

Copy the diagram and fill in the blanks.

Stamps

Look at the stamps. Find out

1 which country is nearest England;
2 which country is furthest from England.

A riddle

My first letter is in **me**.
My second letter is **round**.
My third is in **star**.
My fourth is in **sound**.
My last letter is in **he**.
My whole is a **code**.
What am I?

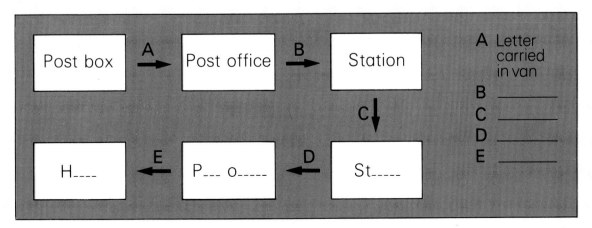

Milk break

It is time for milk in class 1. Keith and Sara are milk monitors. Keith is giving out the milk. The milk crate contains 30 bottles when full. Sara is giving out the straws. Some of the class are finishing their work. The teacher is talking to Andy and Leroy.

Keith and Sara started at table **1**. Then they went clockwise round the room. Miss Price told them to go to the tables at the edge of the room first. Then she told them to go to the tables in the middle. Keith and Sara have just left bottles of milk for Andy and Leroy.

Look at the picture. Then look at the plan. Write answers to these questions.

1 Which tables have got their milk?
2 Which table is next in turn?
3 Which two tables will be last?
4 How many bottles will Keith and Sara leave there?
5 How many bottles have they given out?
6 How many bottles have they still to give out?
7 At which table have they left their own bottles?
8 Will there be any bottles left when they have finished?
9 At which table do Andy and Leroy sit?
10 At which table do Keith and Sara sit?

Puzzle corner

Say which of these sentences are true and which are false.

1 Milk only comes from cows.
2 Milk is only sold in bottles.
3 Milk can be a powder.
4 Margarine is made from milk.
5 Milk is colourless.

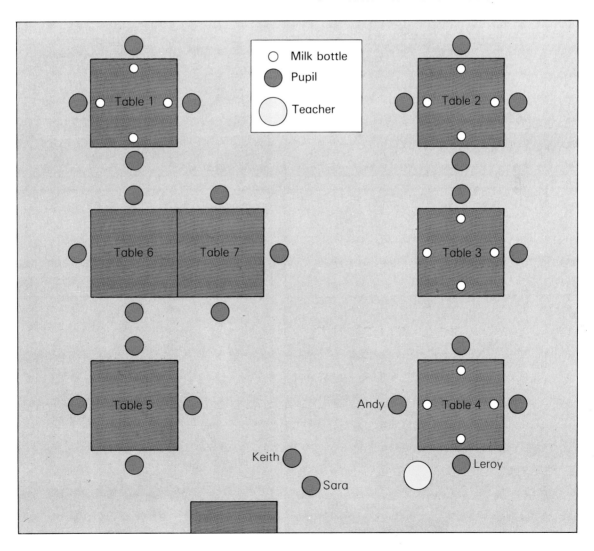

79

Milk tankers

This is the story of a journey. It begins at the dairy and finishes at school. It tells you how class 1 get their bottles of milk.

1 Jeff Anders drives a milk tanker. Every day he calls at ten farms. His job is to collect the milk. Look at the picture. What is Jeff doing? Why must the milk tanker be kept very clean?

3 Jeff has left the main road. He is driving along a lane. Is it wide or narrow? Why must he drive very carefully? What will happen if he meets another lorry?

2 Jeff leaves the dairy at 8 o'clock. He drives to the first farm on his route. Are the farms in the town or the country? Why are the roads busy? Is his tanker empty or full?

4 The second farm he calls at is Ash Farm. It is 9 o'clock. Write some sentences to say what is happening in this picture. Use some of these words to help you: tank, tap, pipe, pumped.

5 The milk has been collected from Ash Farm. It is fresh. The cows were milked at 7 o'clock that morning. How long was the milk in the tank at Ash Farm? Why must Jeff call at the farm every day? How many more farms has he to go to?

7 At the back of the dairy there are railway lines. A train of tankers is lined up. The tanks have been loaded with milk. It is 4 o'clock. The milk that was collected from the farms that morning is being sent to London. Why do you think milk is sent to London? How will it be kept fresh on the journey?

6 By 2 o'clock Jeff is back at the dairy. The milk is being pumped from his tanker into large tanks. It is stored there and kept cool. This helps to keep it fresh. How long has Jeff been away from the dairy? Where has he been?

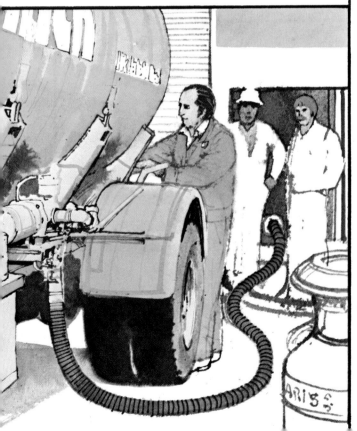

8 Tom drives a milk float. It is used for delivering milk. The milk has been bottled in the dairy. Where is Tom's milk float? What is he carrying on the float besides milk?

Then and now

Look carefully at the two sets of pictures. The pictures on this page show how people got their milk in 1920.

The pictures on page 83 show what happens today. You will see that things have changed between then and now.

Make a list of the numbers 1 to 6. For each number, write a sentence to say what the picture shows for 1920. Then write a sentence to say what today's picture shows. For picture number 1 in 1920, you could write: The cows were milked by hand. For today's picture, you could write: The cows are milked by machine in the milking parlour.

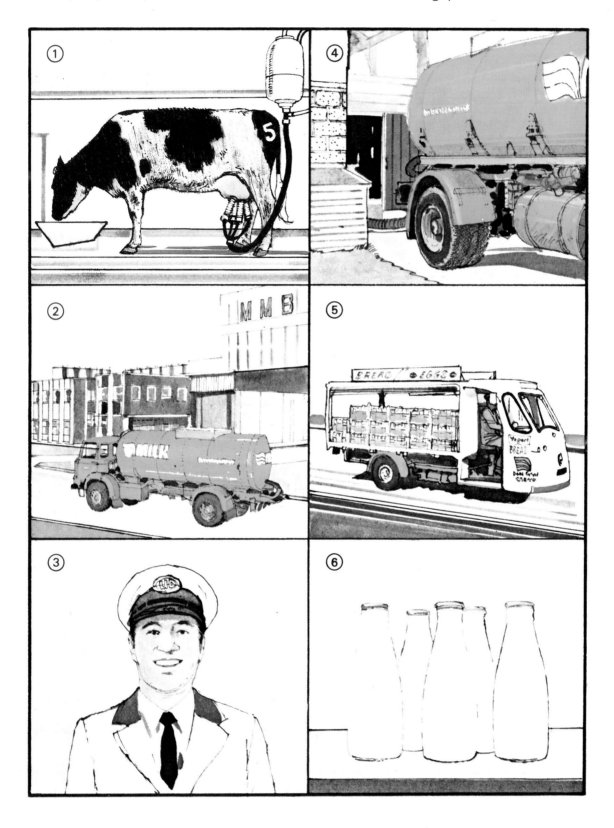

Checking

This is inside a supermarket. In the freezer and on the shelves are things made from milk.

1 Make a list of the things made from milk.

2 Make a list of how each one is packed. These words will help you: tube, carton, box, plastic bottle, glass bottle, paper, tin.

3 Make two headings:
   Stored in the freezer
   Stored on shelves
   Put each item under its correct heading.

4 Why are some things stored in the freezer and not on the shelves?

Milk from farm to home

The diagram shows the journey of milk from farm to home. Copy the numbers **1** to **7**. Write a sentence to describe what is happening in each picture. Add your own title.

Things to do

Next time you go to your local shops or supermarket

1   see how many things you can find that are made from milk,
2   find out the names of four kinds of cheese.

Shapes

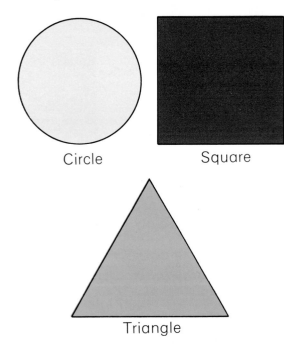

Circle   Square

Triangle

These are the names of some shapes. Look back through the unit. How many of each can you find? Write a sentence about each one.

A mobile

This is a mobile. It is made from milk bottle tops, straws and cotton. Ask your teacher if you can try to make one like it. You could hang it in your bedroom.

Odd one out

Which of these is not made from milk: butter, chocolate, jelly, yogurt?

Make up some puzzles yourself. Try them on your friend.

I scream joke

Why did the raspberry ripple?

Because it saw a banana split.

In the forest

A book, writing paper, a newspaper, a chair, a table, a cupboard – these six things have one thing in common. The title gives you a clue. They are all made from wood. Wood comes from trees. Trees grow in forests. In this unit we will follow some wood on its journey from the forest.

1 This man is a marker. One of his jobs is to choose which trees are to be cut down and to mark them.

2 This man is using a power-saw to cut down the trees. It will take five minutes to fell this tree. It is a dangerous job.

3 This is a special tractor. It is used for pulling the logs out of the forest. The tractor's engine drives a winch. This turns a steel drum which winds in a wire rope. The log is hooked on to the rope.

86

4   This is a fence. The bottom is made of strong wire mesh. At the top there are two rows of wire. The fence is held up by wooden posts. It is about 2 metres high.

5   This stile is used by people who come to the forest for picnics. Children like to play here. Some people are careless. The signs are a warning to them.

6   Some of the trees are cut up into two or three logs. The logs are about 2 metres long. They are stacked in piles, ready to be moved out of the forest.

7   These are special lorries. One has cranes fitted on the back. They are used for lifting the logs on and off the lorry. The other lorry can carry trees up to 10 metres long.

From forest to mill

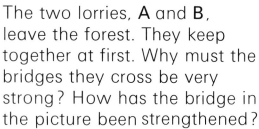

The two lorries, **A** and **B**, leave the forest. They keep together at first. Why must the bridges they cross be very strong? How has the bridge in the picture been strengthened?

Soon the lorries take separate routes. They are both going to different places.

1　Where has lorry **A** gone?
2　Why is it difficult to drive this kind of lorry?
3　What does the sign on the back of lorry **A** say?
4　Why is it there?
5　How will the logs be unloaded?

6　What happens to the logs in the mill?
7　What are the men wearing on their heads?
8　Why are they wearing them?
9　Make a list of dangers in the mill.
10　Will the sawdust be wasted?
11　Name the things made from wood shown in the picture.
12　Find out the names of other things made from wood (a) in your classroom; (b) at home.

1 What happens when lorry **B** meets other traffic on the road?
2 Where has lorry **B** gone?
3 Why must the driver check in at the gates?
4 What is made in this mill?
5 What is another word for mill?
6 What is used in the mill as well as wood?
7 Name the things made from wood pulp shown in the picture.
8 Find out the names of other things made from wood pulp.

Special lorries

The lorries used for carrying logs are specially made for the job. Could an ordinary lorry carry logs 10 metres long?

Look back to page 80. What is the special lorry shown there? In what ways is it special? Make a list of them.

This is another kind of tanker. It carries petrol. Petrol is a dangerous load. What is the main danger of carrying petrol? How are people warned about it?

Imagine you are in a car with your parents driving behind this lorry. The roads are icy. The lorry suddenly starts to skid. It hits a kerb and tips over. What would you do?

Some lorries are specially built to carry new cars. What are they called? How many cars can this lorry carry? Which colour car would be put on the lorry first? Which would be put on last? How are the cars loaded and unloaded? How are the cars kept in place on the lorry? Where have the cars come from? Where do you think they might be going?

This is a cattle waggon. Whose farm is this? Why is there a ramp at the back of the waggon? Why are there holes along the sides? Where might the sheep be going? What other animals could be carried in a cattle waggon?

The tank transporter has to go from Milton to Lee. Look at the picture. Choose which way you would go and say why you have chosen it.

The army uses a lot of special lorries. This is a tank transporter. How do you think the tank is loaded on to the lorry? Why is it necessary to have a crew of three? What is the motor cyclist's job? Could the transporter go down narrow lanes?

A fun lorry

This is a giraffe. Draw a special lorry to take it to a zoo.

Find out the names of some more special lorries. Draw pictures of them and add them to your list.

Longer journeys

This forest is in Canada. Tractors bring their loads of sawn logs from the forest to the water's edge. The logs are tipped into the water.

The man balancing on the logs is a lumberjack. Lumberjacks work in the forest. The lumberjack collects the logs and makes them into a huge raft.

The picture below shows the lumberjack's pole and his boots. The lumberjack also wears thick leather gloves. Sometimes he uses a loudhailer. What are these things used for?

Many of the logs are more than 10 metres long. They are very heavy. But even heavy logs will float in water. Steel chains and ropes link the raft to a powerful boat which pulls it down river to the sawmills and pulp mills.

At the sawmill the bark is stripped off the logs by machines. The logs are then passed through saws to be cut into planks.

Outside the sawmill the planks are stacked in huge piles higher than a house. There are thousands of planks in each pile.

A hundred planks of the same length are made into a bundle. They are fastened together by bands of steel. Fork-lift trucks are used to load the bundles on to a lorry.

The lorry takes them on a short journey to the docks. Here they are loaded on to a waiting ship. In three weeks' time this load of planks will be in England.

Checking

Marking trees

The marker puts paint on every fourth tree in this part of the forest. Copy the plan. Then mark the trees. How many did he mark? How many trees did he leave standing?

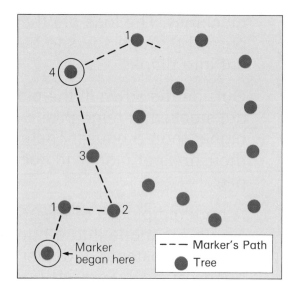

Marker began here
--- Marker's Path
● Tree

Puzzle corner

These trees are so big you can drive a car through them. They are probably the oldest trees in the world. Where are they found? Find out the name of the trees.

Question time

Look back at the pictures on pages 86 and 87.

1   How many trees have been marked?
2   What will happen to them?
3   Why are the men wearing helmets?
4   Which of the jobs being done in the picture is a dangerous one?
5   Small trees are sometimes eaten by animals. Find three different animals in the picture. How are they kept out of the forest?
6   Which machine is used to pull logs out of the forest?
7   How many tools and machines are used in the forest? Make a list of them.
8   Find the box with the white cross. What will it be used for?
9   Who will use the table and benches?
10   Have you visited a forest? If so, write a story or draw a picture about it.

How old?

Every year in a tree's life, a new ring of wood is added to the trunk. You can tell how old a tree is by counting these rings. Each ring is one year's growth. How old was this tree when it was felled?

Journeys

Which is the longer journey, **A** or **B**? Copy out the chart. Look at the pages. Put the answers in the spaces.

	A		B
1	Keith walks to school by road (page 68)		Sara walks to school (page 68)
2	Keith takes the short cut (page 68)		Paul walks to school (page 68)
3	Mr. Burns's post round (page 73)		Letter from America to Westland Road (page 73)
4	Whispers round your class (page 74)		The journey of a letter (page 71)
5	Your journey to school (page 76)		Your friend's journey to school (page 76)
6	Planks from Canada to England (page 93)		Milk from farm to dairy (pages 80 and 81)
7	Sheep from mountain to farm (pages 60 and 61)		Wool from sheep to lorry (pages 62 and 63)
8	Sara's journey round the class (page 78)		Hay from merchant to farm (page 59)
9	Logs from forest to lorry (pages 86 and 87)		Logs from forest to sawmill (pages 88 and 89)
10	Planks from sawmill to docks (page 93)		Planks from Canada to England (page 93)

Puzzle pictures

Look carefully at these pictures. There is a mistake in each one. What is it? Copy the pictures and correct the mistakes.

Synopsis

Oxford New Geography is a complete four-book course for juniors. It introduces the basic skills and concepts of the New Geography at the primary level. The four books are each divided into three sections.

Explorations

How do I find out? How do I record? These and other basic questions are used to develop skills needed by children for a purposeful exploration of the environment. By the use of actual situations children are shown how to look around classroom, school, houses, streets, parks, etc. Familiar situations are used as a springboard for the exploration of less familiar and distant environments.

Face to Face

The emphasis is on presenting lively accounts of people in key occupations as a means of studying the world of work and leisure. Case studies of farms, factories, life in cities and the countryside are used. Children are encouraged to draw comparisons and contrasts with the world they know both at home and abroad.

Links

How are things related and interdependent? From the story of how we get our daily milk and mail to the world of commuters and motorways, the series traces the links that make modern life possible.

The sections contain an average of four units. The units are organized in double-page spreads enabling full use to be made of colour illustrations. The last spread in each unit is used for checking over the work and suggesting lines of further development. Exercises, games and activities cover a wide range of basic geographical skills and concepts.

The Publisher would like to thank the following for permission to reproduce photographs:

Barnaby's Picture Library, p 94; Colorific, p 21; Crown Agents, p 75 (right); Departments of the Environment & Transport, pp 25, 70, 75 (left); PAAT, Oxford, p 85; Jeffrey Tabberner, pp 52, 75, 76, 77.

Illustrated by Sarah De'ath, John Hunt, Peter Jones, Ben Manchipp, Edward McLachlan, Brian Melling, Miller, Craig & Cocking, David Redmond, Tony Richards, Barry Rowe, Simon Stafford, Michael Whittlesea. Cover illustration by Ronald Maddox.

Picture Research by Ann Usborne
Design by Stafford & Stafford, Oxford

First published 1980
Reprinted 1981, 1982, 1987

Oxford University Press, Walton Street, Oxford OX2 6DP

Oxford New York Toronto
Delhi Bombay Calcutta Madras Karachi
Petaling Jaya Singapore Hong Kong Tokyo
Nairobi Dar es Salaam Cape Town
Melbourne Auckland

and associated companies in
Beirut Berlin Ibadan Nicosia

Oxford is a trade mark of Oxford University Press

Filmset by Tradespools Ltd, Frome, Somerset
Printed in Hong Kong

ISBN 0 19 917023 1